All About
Winston Churchill

C. A. Crane

BLUE RIVER PRESS

Indianapolis, Indiana

All About Winston Churchill

Published by Blue River Press
Indianapolis, Indiana
www.brpressbooks.com

Distributed by Cardinal Publishers Group
A Tom Doherty Company, Inc.
www.cardinalpub.com

ISBN: 978-1-68157-098-3

Author: C. A. Crane
Editors: Dani McCormick, Charleen Davis
Interior Illustrators: Bryan Janky, Elizabeth Wells
Book Design: Dave Reed
Cover Artist: Jennifer Mujezinovic
Cover Design: David Miles

Printed in the United States of America

23 22 21 20 19 18 17   1 2 3 4 5 6 7

Contents

Preface   vii

1. Early Childhood   1

2. School Days   10

3. War Correspondent   29

4. Statesman   38

5. Love & Marriage   42

6. Rising Political Star   48

7. WWI Debacle   54

8. Middle East & Russia   59

9. WWII & Prime Minister   64

10. U.S. & WWII   82

11. Post-WWII & Death   93

Select Quotes from Winston Churchill   103

Winston Churchill Timeline   104

World Timeline   105

Glossary   108

Bibliography   112

Index   113

All About
Winston Churchill

Preface

Winston Churchill was arguably the greatest leader and statesman of the twentieth century. He was revered not only in Britain but around the world. He is perhaps best known for his politics and for serving as a beacon of light during World War II. He saw early on how evil Adolf Hitler and the Nazis were, but it took some time for others to follow his lead. His alliance with America under President Franklin D. Roosevelt was key to winning the war.

Churchill was also a famous author and painter. He was awarded the Nobel Prize for Literature in 1953. He is still discussed today, and people quote him or mention him in books, speeches, movies, and TV shows. Churchill is very much alive in people's minds and imaginations, and they point to him when they desire their politicians to live up to Churchill's example of extraordinary leadership.

He holds a special place in the hearts of many Americans as well. President John F. Kennedy awarded an honorary U.S. citizenship to Churchill in 1963. Winston was a master of words and a man of abundant wit and wisdom. His ability to inspire, lead with confidence and conviction, and take responsibility for his actions defined his character. People admired how he defended his moral and ethical principles and appreciated his good-hearted nature. He did his best to not hold grudges or seek revenge, and always tried to genuinely enjoy life. Altogether, that is what makes him one of the most popular and admired figures of our time.

Chapter 1
<u>Early Childhood</u>

Winston grew up at Bleinheim Palace
and liked to play on the lawn

On November 30, 1874 in Blenheim Palace in England, Winston Leonard Spencer Churchill was born. Winston was from a prominent English family line (Spencer-Churchill) from his father's side. Lord Randolph Churchill, Winston's father, was the third son of the seventh Duke of Marlborough.

Winston's roots were also half American. His mother, the beautiful socialite Jennie Jerome, was from Brooklyn, New York. She was the second oldest of four sisters. Her father, Leonard, was a wealthy American banker and founded

As a baby, Winston did not show any hint
that he would one day be world famous

the American Jockey Club that registered
Thoroughbred horses. Jennie attended school
mainly in Paris. She was well-known in European
social circles, and when Lord Randolph met
her it was love at first sight. Jennie's social
contacts greatly enhanced Lord Randolph's
political career.

From ages two to six, Winston lived in Dublin,
Ireland, where his grandfather was a Viceroy,
an appointed official of the British monarchy.
His job was to help the King govern Ireland,
and Winston's father worked as his secretary.
Winston loved to watch the parades and was

fascinated by the extravagant celebrations that he saw in Ireland.

Winston's grandfather the seventh Duke of Marlborough was appointed by the King of England to help rule Ireland

As a toddler, living in a house called "The Little Lodge," he ran and hid in the bushes when he heard a teacher was coming to begin "education." He had to learn how to read without crying. Winston also had to do math by hand; there were no calculators or computers. Once he finished one worksheet, another one followed. Winston said, "There appeared to be no limits to these." Lessons kept him from more fun activities that he wanted to do.

In 1879, the family moved back to England. Winston didn't have many friends his age because he moved around so much. He had adult friends that told him stories. He was particularly attracted to stories that centered on wars and soldiers.

Winston's parents were Englishman Lord Randolph Churchill and American Jennie Jerome

When he was four, Winston watched the HMS Eurydice capsize. The boat had been badly damaged by a storm and sank near the Isle of Wight. All but two of the crew died. There was little anyone could do to save the people aboard, which bothered Winston.

Lord Randolph, Winston's father, was a politician. He held various positions, such as Secretary of State for India, Leader of the House of Commons, and Chancellor of the Exchequer. He fought hard for his Conservative Party. He seemed poised to be the Prime Minister, but a number of political blunders and a misunderstanding led to his resignation at a relatively young age.

Because his father was so busy, he didn't spend much time with Winston, which was hard on the young boy. However, Winston loved and greatly respected his father. Winston would often defend him if he was mocked in the press or if Winston overheard any hurtful comments. Winston learned from his father and tried to earn his respect. Winston seemed to finally get closer to his father when he attended a military academy and began moving up and gaining accolades.

His mother Jennie saw to Winston's education and helped to provide him with opportunities to build his professional and social life, which already had a strong foundation because of his family's prestige. Both his parents sent him books when he was away at school, but they remained distant. As a boy, Winston put his parents on a

Young Winston was not seen as a scholar and was often underestimated by adults

pedestal. He once said that his mother "always seemed to me a fairy princess: a radiant being possessed of limitless riches and power." "She shone for me like the Evening Star. I loved her dearly—but at a distance."

Winston was very close to his nanny, Mrs. Everest, a modest woman who was like a second mother to him and cherished him. Winston once wrote, "[She] was my confidante. Mrs. Everest . . . looked after me and tended all my wants. It was to her I poured out my many troubles, both now and in schooldays."

He received much of his religious education from her. One could say Winston was respectful of religious beliefs, but personally did not like all the rules that came with religion. He more closely aligned himself with the Low Church, which was more informal, than the High Church, which followed strict rules.

When Mrs. Everest was no longer needed in the household, Winston's parents let her go. Winston did not think they took good enough care of her. Although just a boy, he sent her money whenever he could. Winston always had a picture of Mrs. Everest hanging in the room wherever he worked, even when he had grown to be a powerful figure in Britain.

Winston's mother was a beautiful, wealthy woman who thoroughly enjoyed her social life in England

Winston had one sibling, a younger brother name John Strange Spencer Churchill, who was called Jack. They were always close, and Winston confided in his brother. As an adult, Jack and his sons even went with Winston once to America. Winston's role in public life simply overshadowed Jack in history.

Winston loved his nanny Elizabeth Everest who was like a mother to him

Chapter 2
School Days

At age six, Winston had to leave home to go to St. George's School. Winston called it St. James's School in his book about his early life, probably because he did not have good things to say about the school. He had to leave behind all of his toys and everything familiar to him to move alone to a strange place and live with people he did not know. In Winston's time, this was more common for children in noble families or families with money.

Adults told him that schools were much nicer now than when they attended. St. George's School was an impressive place, and Winston was told it was luxurious. It had electricity, so compared to other schools, it was like a vacation. His older cousins who had gone away to school did not let on that it was not at all like a vacation. Instead, boys who misbehaved were hit with a stick. At the time Winston attended, the head of the school was particularly strict about punishment. If they did something bad enough, boys would get caned for misbehaving.

St. George's School looked impressive
but was run by a strict headmaster

Winston's mother Jennie dropped him off with no visible concern. Soon, Winston was miserable. He did not get very far in his studies in the two years he was at St. George's. Winston was full of anxiety, but reading nourished him and kept him going. He hungrily read *Treasure Island*, a present from his father. Winston's teachers were perplexed by him. He read way above his age, but still did not do well in school. Winston wrote, "My teachers saw me at once backward and precocious." No matter how he was forced, he could not learn what did not interest him.

Winston received few visits from his parents. He also described the cruelty of his school. These factors probably contributed to Winston falling ill and leaving St. George's. Winston claimed that he nearly died of double pneumonia. While recovering from illness, he attended a smaller school in Brighton that was run by two women. The atmosphere was more friendly and easygoing than his previous school. He got to study subjects that he enjoyed, such as history, poetry, and horseback riding. Winston said later that he thought giving boys horses was more useful than giving them money. The outdoors and fresh air in Brighton helped Winston grow stronger. This school suited him, and he stayed for three years.

Winston said about this time, "I was now embarked on a military career. This orientation was entirely due to my collection of [toy] soldiers. I had ultimately nearly fifteen hundred." Lord Randolph was impressed by Winston's set up of the toy troops. He asked Winston if he wanted to go into the army. Winston was only a young boy and thought leading an army would be fabulous. After displaying his army men in correct formation to his father, Winston's studies became geared toward getting into The Royal Military Academy.

Winston impressed his father with intricate arrangements of his toy soldiers

As a teenager, it was decided that Winston would not attend his father's high school, Eton College. Instead, Winston attended Harrow School, a boarding school for boys aged thirteen to eighteen, but he remained at the bottom of his class. At twelve-years-old, Winston got into Harrow School. He did terribly on the entrance exams, the first he had ever taken. They tested him on subjects that he found boring, and he could not understand the Latin, so he just scribbled a bit on his paper and was done. He was admitted, but at a low level.

When Winston was thirteen, his father resigned as Leader of the House of Commons and Chancellor of the Exchequer. Since Winston's father was a well-known politician, people visited the school just to watch Winston line up for roll call. They were surprised and whispered rude comments about Winston being nearly last in his class, as indicated by his position at the end of the line.

Winston was strong in the face of criticism. He looked forward and did not worry about what people said about him. He was attending Harrow to learn and was not embarrassed by not knowing some things. He loved the songs, special lectures, and speakers at Harrow.

Winston attended Harrow as a teenager
and found he was talented in speech and writing

His parents did not come to Harrow often, which disappointed Winston. He constantly wrote letters to his parents, especially his mother, begging for visits. He even scolded her for not coming to see him. She liked to travel and often left on trips, though seldom to Harrow. His father was also wrapped up in his own life. His parents did write him some harsh, critical letters about his conduct and doing poorly in his studies. They wanted him to follow a path more suitable to his upbringing and social standing. Winston's brother, Jack, was better at fitting the mold, and gave his parents little trouble.

Winston did not like to study much and was never good at Latin. The Reverend J.E.C. Welldon, who would later become a friend, was headmaster at Harrow and made faces whenever Winston tried to pronounce Latin words. He even tried to tutor Winston in Latin for a term, but finally had to give up.

Winston reveled in learning English, which was considered beneath learning Latin or Greek, but certainly served Winston well throughout his life. Soon Winston's mastery of English turned into a real gift for speech and writing that would support him all his life.

At one point, Winston traded expertise with a fellow student. Winston would help his friend, who was in a higher grade, write essays if he helped Winston with Latin translations. This plan was thwarted when the boys nearly were found out. One day, Winston's friend was praised by the headmaster for his fine essay. The headmaster then started asking him about some of the contents of his essay. He was nervous and, of course, could not talk much about the essay. He just scraped by, and Winston thought that maybe their plan was not such a good one after all.

Winston and Jack often played together
with their dog during school breaks

Winston was not a great student, but he had a superb memory. He was good at memorizing literature and geography, and passed an exam to enlist in the Army while other boys his age did not. Winston seemed particularly suited to the military.

After three years at Harrow, he took a class on the army to prepare to attend the Cadet School at The Royal Military Academy, Sandhurst (RMAS), usually referred to simply as Sandhurst. British Army officers are trained at the school. It took him three tries to be accepted to the school.

Frustrated at being unsuccessful in getting into Sandhurst a first and second time, Winston enrolled in a "cramming" school that had a good track record with teaching its enrollees how to succeed in taking exams. As Winston prepared to attend, he had a horrible accident.

Winston was eighteen, and his brother Jack was twelve. They were in the countryside staying at an aunt's estate and playing chase with their cousins. When Winston was just about to be caught by the other two boys on a bridge—his brother and his cousin were on either side— he made a calculated decision to jump off the bridge. He grabbed pine branches on his descent, but was unable to stop the fall. It was a nearly thirty-foot drop, and Winston was knocked unconscious when he hit the ground. Winston was confined to bed for three months and was not in good shape for a year.

On his third try at the entrance exams, Winston finally got into Sandhurst. At Sandhurst, he enjoyed and excelled in the practical applications of what he was learning. He collected military books and histories to read to supplement his regular studies. He hated mathematics, and left it behind once he got into Sandhurst. He thought highly of mathematicians, though, and was glad that other people, like engineers, found math useful.

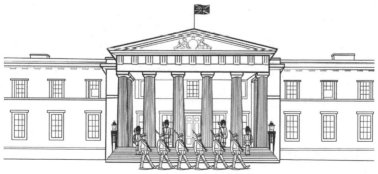

Winston never gave up and on his
third try was admitted to Sandhurst

Winston enjoyed Sandhurst and remarked that he was not held back because of his "past neglect of Latin, French, or Mathematics." Instead, all of the students had to learn new subjects. Winston and his fellow students took classes in tactics, fortification, mapmaking, military law, and military administration. They were required to work on their drills, gymnastics, and riding skills too. Winston enjoyed riding, but disliked drills. He liked the rest of his classes, though, and did well.

Unlike Winston's previous schools, where students were required to play on a sports team, at Sandhurst, no one had to play a sport unless they wanted to. Winston chose to play polo with his friends, and kept a couple of ponies for that reason. Winston had many friends from his Sandhurst years, but friends from military school rarely last. By the time Winston published a memoir of his early life in 1930, thirty-six years after his graduation, many of his friends had been injured. A number of his friends died in war.

While at Sandhurst, Winston got a lesson in politics, an area which would eventually be the main focus of his life. In 1894, Winston saw an advertisement in the *Daily Telegraph* for a meeting to organize a group of citizens, The Entertainments Protection League, to fight against the Purity Campaign, headed by Mrs. Laura Ormiston Chant from the county government. Her main obsession was cleaning up the theaters: in particular, The Empire.

Winston was not on Mrs. Chant's side and did not see that anything needed cleaning up to protect people against bad influences. He wrote to the man who was organizing the league and said he wanted to participate. The organizer wrote back on fancy stationery and invited Winston to an evening meeting. He prepared a speech, which he practiced and memorized. When he arrived at the meeting after a long train ride into London, only the organizer was there. Nobody else had bothered. The organizer fumed about how Brits had gotten too apathetic, and had lost their fighting spirit.

Both men were disappointed. When Winston left, he had to make his way back to Sandhurst, but was short on money. He had to sell a watch that his father had given him in order to have enough money to buy some food and take the train. He said that it was the last, and the only, time that he would do such a thing. He was always careful to have enough money to take care of himself and cover his expenses.

Eventually, Mrs. Chant was partially successful, and lightweight screens were erected

Winston took a train to and from Sandhurst to meet with a man who was organizing to fight against the Purity Campaign

between places that sold alcohol, making it harder for customers to readily move between them. One evening, a group of mostly upper-class men got rowdy and started to pull down the flimsy screens. Winston was part of the crowd. Seizing the moment, he stood on a makeshift platform and finally made the speech he had memorized. He edited it a bit to appeal to the crowd. This was Winston's first official speech. He spoke against the government controlling people's habits and social pleasures.

The crowd reacted enthusiastically to his speech. The story of this event appeared in the

Winston's first speech was given to a group of people protesting the Purity Campaign

newspapers. This event gave Winston added confidence in his preparation and memorization skills. Unfortunately the government seemed intimidated by Mrs. Chant and her followers and shortly erected sturdy brick barriers between the bars.

Shortly after his impromptu lesson on public speaking, Winston graduated from Sandhurst. He was often at the bottom of his classes at the schools he attended, although at Sandhurst, he finished eighth in his class in 1894. Sandhurst suited Winston, but graduating and leaving Sandhurst suited him even more, as the adventures that awaited him were the most thrilling of his life.

Winston observed that those in charge and teaching the students at Sandhurst were serious army men, but also human and able to bend. They were not always strict to the letter. His father, with whom Winston always longed for a closer father-son relationship, looked at Winston more favorably when he became a gentleman cadet.

Colonel Brabazon, a handsome intelligent soldier who was friends with Winston's parents, wanted Winston to join his army regiment as a cavalry officer. At that time, being a cavalry officer meant Winston had to pay for his horse and uniforms, which were both expensive. Winston's father said no, but his mother thought it was fine. As his father's health worsened, he interfered less with Winston's life and his desire to join the regiment. Eventually, Lord Randolph acted genuinely happy that Winston would be a cavalry officer.

On January 24, 1895, when Winston was twenty-years-old, his father died at age forty-six of a strange illness. Winston wrote, "All of my dreams of comradeship with him, of entering Parliament at his side and in his support, were ended. There remained for me only to pursue his aims and vindicate his memory."

Winston's father was formidable and distant, but he and Winston loved each other. He died before Winston could know whether or not their relationship would have deepened, but Winston thought it would have. In the coming years, Winston would pen a biography commemorating his father and, in part, to set the record straight about his political career.

Winston's father had made good investments, but he had many debts, and everything had to be sold to clear them. Winston felt an

Winston was proud to join the cavalry
after graduating from Sandhurst

urgency to find a career path and a way to make money. He was a superb writer and speaker, and writing provided him with money, starting in his twenties. At the time of his father's death, Winston's mother was just forty-years-old, energetic and youthful. She helped Winston in whatever way she could to encourage him and move his plans along. Winston said she became more like a sister to him.

Lord Randolph's death at forty-six inspired Winston to write his father's biography

Two months later, in March 1895, Winston was assigned to the army regiment the Fourth Hussars under Brabazon and became a lieutenant. In this same year, Winston's beloved Mrs. Everest became ill and he rushed to see her in London and to consult with doctors. He spent some time with this service-oriented, caring woman, and she died peacefully. He made sure that she had a proper tombstone and paid for the upkeep of her grave.

Later, when Winston was in Parliament, he supported creating pensions for older people that would help them financially in their old age. In this way, he was able to help seniors have a more secure life than Mrs. Everest had. Mrs. Everest gave Winston her affection and support throughout his childhood and youth. Without her love and understanding, Winston's childhood would have been quite unhappy.

Chapter 3
War Correspondent

Winston liked excitement. There were no active wars in Britain at the time, and Winston craved action. His mother arranged a job for him working as a war correspondent-officer in Cuba. He wrote articles for the *Daily Graphic* newspaper but didn't give up his commission as a soldier. This was uncommon, but not unheard of, and Winston and his mother were known to push limits. Winston humorously wrote about his mother's ongoing influence: "In my interest [my mother] left no wire unpulled, no stone unturned, no cutlet uncooked."

Winston's love for America began with his first trip to New York City

Before cars, a two wheeled closed carriage
was a common mode of transportation

Before leaving for Cuba, however, he went on his first trip to America. At this time in New York City, one saw horses and carriages, not cars. Winston had been told that the city was expensive and he would be bored, but Winston found otherwise. Family connections made it possible for Winston to be entertained in high style, attending parties with Astors and Rockefellers, prominent families in America. Winston loved his time in America, and this visit was one of many he would make in his life. Winston came to think of America as a second home.

When Winston left America for Cuba, he was heading into a war zone. He fought under General Álvaro Suárez Valdéz against Máximo Gómez, who was leading the Cuban rebels against Spain. Winston first experienced fighting on his twenty-first birthday. He later wrote that "on that day, for the first time, I heard shots fired in anger and heard bullets strike flesh or whistle through the air." Winston escaped getting hit, sometimes narrowly. He sent reports of the fighting to the press.

Winston knew that those who had been engaged in war were respected, looked up to, and envied. Those who had not been a part of any conflict wanted to be. Winston had finally gotten his chance while in Cuba. He was under fire and stayed in squalid places, with sickness everywhere.

The next five years, from 1895 to 1900, Winston sought out, observed, or fought in wars as a correspondent-officer. While doing this, he got paid for his writings about the military campaigns and accumulated medals. Winston said this period in his life was his real education. He learned a lot by traveling, meeting new people, and witnessing war.

Winston discovered Havana cigars while in Cuba, which appeared regularly with Winston in photos afterwards. Winston's ever-present cigar became a part of his iconic image.

In 1897, Winston took off to India, again as a war correspondent-officer. Britain had been in India for a long time, and from 1858 to 1947, India was actually a colony of Britain. The British Army had trained a group of locals to be soldiers and guard Khyber Pass. The Pass was a path through the mountains that let the British come and go from India easier.

However, a group of people native to the area ambushed the soldiers and captured the Pass. They knew the landscape better and had more people, so the British had to be careful. It took a lot of time to plan how to get the Pass back.

In Winston's downtime while waiting for action, he eagerly read books on many subjects.

Winston served in the cavalry in many different places like Cuba, India, Egypt, and Sudan

He always wanted to keep learning and seeking knowledge. His steel-trap memory helped him to do so. Based on his experience fighting a frontier war in India, he soon published the first of his many books, *The Story of the Malakand Field Force.*

He next fought in Egypt as a correspondent-officer. Egypt was struggling under high taxes, and some of the people in Egypt-controlled Sudan revolted, resulting in an eighteen year-long war. In 1898, Winston witnessed the brutal Battle of Omdurman. The new weapons of Britain overpowered the opposition. Winston did not shy away from describing the gruesome violence of battle in his writings. A reader needs a strong stomach to read these realistic accounts!

At the end of 1898, Winston finally returned to England after resigning from the British Army. He wanted to attend Oxford University but found that he did not have the educational requirements needed; again his deficiency in Latin and Greek was a problem. So he turned to politics and ran his first race for a place in the House of Commons. He was swiftly defeated, but was admired for his ardent campaigning. During this time, Winston began to write his book *The River War*, based on his experience in the Sudan, and it was published within the year.

On October 11, 1899, the South African War, also called the Second Boer War, began. Winston left England again, this time as a civilian journalist instead of an officer. He was just twenty-four and had already been involved in his fifth war campaign.

The Boer wars were in South Africa, but were fought by Europeans. Winston shipped out as soon as he could so that he could be a part of the action.

CAPE OF GOOD HOPE

The Cape Colony fought Transvaal in the Second Boer War, with the Orange Free State between them

A month later in November, Winston was with a scouting group on a mission in an armored train. The Boers, against whom the Brits were fighting, attacked the train. Winston's take-charge attitude kicked in. Even though he wasn't a soldier, he maintained a military stance and gave orders, keeping everyone motivated. Winston jumped off the train to make sure no one was left behind. It was then that he was captured and taken to jail in Pretoria. He told his captors he was not a soldier, but a war correspondent. They took him to jail anyway.

Winston hated confinement. He escaped from the jail, and a generous reward was offered by the Boers for his capture. They described Winston by saying he had a "small, hardly noticeable mustache, talks through his nose, and cannot pronounce the letter S properly." Although it was dangerous for anyone to help him, he was hidden on a train that would take him to safety. Then he traveled on a small boat to Durban, a large city in Cape Colony, where he was welcomed like a hero.

Winston had shown incredible ingenuity and bravery. His capture and escape altered

the course of his life by getting him national
attention, which he liked. His name and picture
were everywhere.

At age twenty-four, Winston was captured
after jumping off a train in enemy territory

Chapter 4
Statesman

Winston had written several books by age twenty-six
and went on an extensive lecture tour

When Winston returned to England, illustrious and a folk hero, he turned to politics again. In fall 1900, he ran to be a representative for the Oldham district in the House of Commons as a Conservative and won. By this time, at age twenty-six, he had already written and published one novel and four nonfiction books—one in 1898, one in 1899, and three in

1900—that centered on wars he was in. They were often based on the articles he had written for newspapers. He capitalized on his popularity by going on a paid lecture tour that included America from December through February.

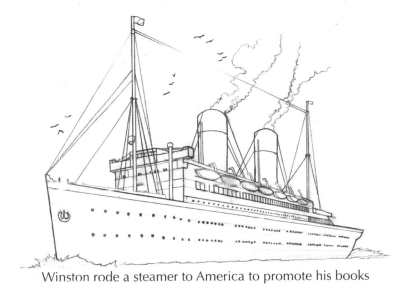

Winston rode a steamer to America to promote his books

When he arrived in America for the second time by steamer, reporters met him. Winston jokingly said, "I am not here to marry anybody." He was poking fun at the rise of marriages between wealthy Americans and titled British. The Americans were a bit lukewarm to Winston, as they had differing feelings about the South

African War. Many voiced their opinion that they were on the side of the Boers, the underdogs.

Winston had to win the audiences over, which he did with his quick wit and knack for choosing the right words. He admitted admiration for the Boers and said they were formidable in their fight for independence. The audiences warmed up to him and he found them generally welcoming.

Boston was the focus of this trip. There he met the American writer, Winston Churchill, whose name he shared. The two had exchanged humorous letters back and forth across the ocean, and they had arrived at a formal agreement about how their names would appear on their books. Winston would use his full name, and the other suggested adding "the American" after his name. The *Boston Herald* featured them on the front page of the newspaper: "Namesakes meet. Winston Churchills Fast Friends." They found they had much in common. Both were in their twenties and had found success at a relatively young age. Although they searched, they never found a common relative between them.

Winston met many notable Americans during this tour. At his lecture in the Waldorf Astoria ballroom in New York City, he was introduced by the famous author Mark Twain, then in his sixties, whose work Winston had admired when he was young. Twain signed a collection of his work containing twenty-five volumes for Winston.

In February 1901, upon his return to Britain from abroad, he gave a speech and took his seat in the House of Commons. Winston's lucrative writing career made his life in politics possible. By this time, Winston had accumulated more than $60,000 from his lectures and five published books. At age twenty-six, his official life in politics began.

Winston would not return to the United States for nearly thirty years.

One of the highlights of Winston's trip to America was meeting famous author Mark Twain

Chapter 5
Love & Marriage

Winston had an active social life, but his ambitions did not include running after women. Then in 1904, Winston was introduced to Clementine Hozier. Winston's mother knew Clementine's mother because their families had mutual friends. Winston was struck by Clementine's good looks, and continued to stare at her, much to her annoyance. Neither was much impressed overall with the other, and Winston did not speak, but that was only the first time they met.

In 1908 at a dinner party, they had more time to connect. Winston asked Clementine if she had read the book he had published about his father. She had not. He promised to send it to her, but he forgot. Clementine was not amused.

After Winston spent time with Clementine again, he was taken by her intelligence and good nature. In the four years they had not seen each other, Clementine had gotten engaged twice to the same man, but had broken it off. Winston had proposed to other women, supposedly including the American actress Ethel Barrymore, but had been turned down.

Winston's and Clementine Hozier's romance
did not begin with love at first sight

Although many of the women who pursued Winston were ultra-wealthy, he preferred Clementine. He valued contentment more than money. He loved Clementine, and she loved him. In 1908, Winston invited her to his family home at Blenheim Palace. Winston wanted to ask Clementine to marry him, but he was very nervous and kept delaying. He had to be encouraged by his cousin to get on with it. He finally proposed when they were walking in the garden. Clementine accepted. She was twenty-three, ten years younger than Winston.

Four years after their first meeting,
Winston and Clementine wed
in St. Margaret's Church, Westminster

Winston was a complex man. He was imaginative and a creative genius; artistic with a practical side. Clementine balanced him; she gave Winston solid and mostly correct advice. He and Clementine were well-suited. Winston and Clementine married in September 1908.

Their marriage was successful for many reasons. They had common goals, and both had a social life tied to politics and advancement. They were not always together, but enjoyed each other's company when they were, and were loyal to each other.

Winston was never known as a ladies' man. He met and spent time with beautiful, charismatic women in his busy, public, and long life, but he was not interested in romance with them. He was faithful to Clementine. Gossip did not follow Winston.

Winston and Clementine were deeply devoted to each other and wrote letters when they were apart. Sometimes Winston wrote four per day! They even wrote notes to each other when they were in the same house. Sometimes the letters included drawings. They addressed each other with pet names; he was 'Pug' and she was 'Cat.' Their good marriage was remarkable among marriages of the elite of that time, especially considering infidelity ran in their families. To the outside world, Clementine's father was the late Colonel Sir Henry Hozier. Clementine's real father is not known, but it was likely not Hozier.

Winston and Clementine had five children: Diana, born in 1909; Randolph in 1911; and Sarah in 1914. In 1918, Marigold was born, but died when she was almost three from septicemia. Clementine and Winston were grief stricken, but they drew closer from this loss. Their last child, Mary, was born in 1922.

Winston cherished Chartwell,
which remained his home until he died

Shortly after Mary's birth, they bought the house, Chartwell, in Kent, an area Winston loved since he was a boy. This love probably began with his governess Mrs. Everest, who held it in high regard. It was not until two years later that they were able to move in because the house needed work. It became a place of solace for Winston, especially in stressful times. Winston liked change and travel, to see with his own eyes places all over the globe, but he always liked returning to Chartwell. His family lived at Chartwell the rest of Winston's life.

Winston often retreated to Chartwell to be with his family

Chapter 6
Rising Political Star

Winston was somewhat a rebel in government. He did not like to be fixed into a box. He was a rising star in the Conservative Party. Winston wanted free trade and less taxes on imports, but his party was in disagreement. So, Winston switched from the Conservative to the Liberal Party in 1904. This would be one of many switches.

Winston served as a Member of the House of Commons in the Parliament

Between 1906 and 1911, Winston served in various posts. In The House of Commons, the politicians had lively debates. They gave long, engaging speeches and argued with each other. He deeply respected the traditions of the Commons and enjoyed his job. He had a real concern for the common man, and was a frontrunner for welfare reform.

Winston introduced social changes, such as an eight-hour workday, the National Insurance Act (1911) that provided unemployment aid and help for children, and Acts that helped miners and shop assistants. Lloyd George, who was the Chancellor of the Exchequer at this time, was often the powerhouse behind the reforms. He controlled the money. He and Winston frequently worked in partnership for reform.

Winston had many enduring friendships, though Clementine was not always fond of his choices. One friend she particularly disliked was F.E. Smith, a Member of Parliament. Winston enjoyed entertaining, and he and Smith talked, debated, and laughed until all hours of the night. Winston said Smith was the only person who exceeded him in brain power. They created "The Other Club" to gather a flock of friends, including politicians and those outside politics, for fun, food, and conversation. The club thrived.

Winston formed "The Other Club,"
a sort of social think tank, with his friends

In 1911, Winston was promoted to First Lord of the Admiralty to strengthen the Navy. He had use of the yacht, *The Enchantress*, complete with a crew. Winston spent nearly eighteen months checking out the naval bases. As he did most of his life, he worked day and night. He learned everything he could and quickly. He had to ensure the Navy was always ready and prepared for war.

The British then were most concerned about German attacks. Winston had a no-nonsense character and broad vision. He studied the military apparatus of Germany and France, two of Britain's neighboring countries. Winston was concerned because Germany had a topnotch army, but Britain still had a large navy. He feared war was on the horizon.

Winston enjoyed use of *The Enchantress*, a luxurious yacht

Winston revered the past battle tactics and military spectacle, but Winston looked to the future. The world was changing as the Industrial Revolution raged. New technology was constantly being created and Winston wanted Britain to be part of the action, whatever it might be. He was fascinated by technology—warships, artilleries, power and speed—and pushed for the development of the tank. Winston saw and understood both the advantages and dangers of technological advancement.

Winston argued with the older military men while trying to construct new and better battleships and destroyers to be able to compete with Germany. He got the fleet ready, but when the war he predicted came, it hurt him on many levels. Winston had foreseen its miseries and was prepared, but not enthusiastic.

In 1914, the Great War, which is now known as World War I, broke out. The spark that started it was the assassination in Bosnia of Archduke Franz Ferdinand of the Austro-Hungarian Empire. This brought all the problems in Europe to the surface. Borders and resources had been a long-term dispute among some countries. People hoped that peace would prevail, but Austria-Hungary declared war on Serbia, the home of the assassin. Quickly, Great Britain, France, Russia, and Belgium allied with Serbia against Austria-Hungary and its ally Germany. World War I had begun.

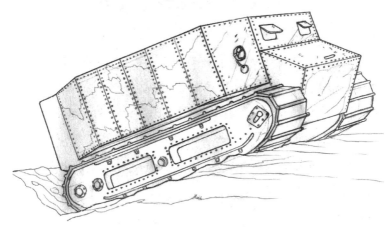

Winston pushed the military to develop new technology, like tanks

Many people, including Winston, thought the war would be over quickly. This was not to be. The war lasted for four years. WWI was disastrous and problems arose from it well into the next century.

Chapter 7
WWI Debacle

In 1914, Winston was still First Lord of the Admiralty. Winston enjoyed this position, but he perhaps needed more time and experience to better fit the job. As Winston knew, when you are in the position to make hard decisions, you live with the consequences, good or bad. He came up with a plan to try to win the war quickly called the Gallipoli Campaign.

Winston was promoted to First Lord of the Admiralty in 1911 and perhaps needed more experience for this job

WWI was raging in Europe, and Britain and France had lost many men. In 1915, in order to try to change the gridlock of the war, Winston planned an invasion in the Gallipoli Peninsula in Turkey to gain control of the waters. His strategy included a naval attack through the Dardanelles. The cabinet was in favor, and Lloyd George wanted a combined effort of the Navy and Army.

In the Gallipoli Campaign, British Forces tried to take over the Gallipoli peninsula to gain control of the Dardanelles, a narrow stretch of water between Europe and Turkey

Winston thought the Navy could handle it alone. This maneuver did not work and ended up in slaughter of the Allied forces. The conflict continued for nine months until all Allied troops cleared out. Winston was plagued politically by it for a long time, and his political opponents did not let him forget, but he learned from his mistakes. By the time of the next world war (WWII), he was well-prepared for any challenge. Winston always remembered the Dardanelles and tried not to repeat his failure.

In 1916, after the Dardanelles debacle, Winston was removed from the Admiralty post. Confidence in him had been lost, and the Conservative Party wanted him out of the Admiralty post. Rightly or not, Winston was blamed for all the bloodshed. His impatience may have cost around 200,000 British lives.

Winston was demoted to a minor post and relieved of most of his responsibilities. He felt he was a pawn, and that his political career might be finished, so he resigned from government. The "black dog" that Winston called depression or dark moods now afflicted him. It would do so throughout his life, but he continually conquered it.

Winston felt ruined, but he fought his way back, as always. He escaped by going to war. He became a soldier in the trenches in Flanders, Belgium, where he commanded a battalion. He wasn't exactly welcomed after the Dardanelles catastrophe, yet the men began to like him. Winston was willing to be in the midst of action, sharing all the dangers to fight alongside his men. He also enjoyed leisure time with them.

As a soldier in Flanders,
Winston worked to reignite his reputation

He wrote often to Clementine, who supported him. This enabled Winston to bounce back from his grief over the Dardanelles campaign. He also started painting, which he would continue to do throughout his life. Winston had seen his sister-in-law painting in water colors. She let him borrow the paints, and a neighbor gave him some brief instruction and advice. Winston quickly realized he was good at it.

Painting could be added to his list of talents and allowed him to focus on his art when he needed relief from other concerns. His first painting was "The Garden at Hoe Farm." Perhaps not surprisingly, Winston eventually gained notoriety for his colorful paintings, and although he did not paint to make money, he, his family, and charities ended up receiving lots of money for his work. Over the course of nearly fifty years, he painted over 500 paintings.

Chapter 8
Middle East & Russia

In 1917, Winston returned to government. A new leader was in charge; Lloyd George of the Liberal Party was now Prime Minister. Lloyd had always dominated Winston, but they had respect for one another and worked together well. Lloyd wanted Winston back. He asked Winston to be Minister of Munitions (head of weaponry), which proved to be a wise move.

It did not take long for Winston to clean up and streamline operations in an office that had become bogged down with bureaucracy. Winston dramatically improved the type and quantity of supplies, weapons, and ammunition, and visited the front to check on everything. Many people were once again impressed with Winston.

Trouble was everywhere. In 1917, there was disorder in India and Turkey (formerly part of the Ottoman Empire). In Russia, the people overthrew the government in an uprising called the Bolshevik Revolution. In the Bolshevik Revolution, the Czar and the entire family was killed, and a communist state was created. After the Revolution, Russia changed its name to the Soviet Union.

Britain was concerned about the Bolshevik Revolution for two reasons. First, the Romanovs, the royal family of Russia, were actually related to the royal family of England. They were cousins! Second, communism could spread from Russia and begin toppling other world governments. Winston wanted to stop the spread of communism, so he sent troops. However, Winston was too late and the Bolshevik Revolution was too far along. The British operation was halted when it did not appear to be succeeding.

Some believed that, had Winston's campaign succeeded, millions of Russians may have been saved from death, and dictators such as Mussolini and Hitler may never have gotten into power. Winston remained anti-communist and warned against communism most of his life. He regretted that Britain had not stopped it. Because Winston was very vocal and front and center on this matter, he was an easy target for blame by his critics for not defeating communism early on.

Winston did not worry. Instead he turned his attention to the Middle East where Britain wanted to find a shared policy. Winston created a new Middle East Department that held a conference in Cairo in 1921. This was one of many meetings of high-level officials he would arrange over his career.

T.E. Lawrence, also known as Lawrence of Arabia, a Brit that helped lead Arab rebels, served as Winston's advisor at the conference. Lawrence spoke Arabic, cared greatly about the Arabs, and was a British Army officer. He spoke up for the Arabic people and tried to do what was best for everyone. Winston and he became friends. They wrote letters to each other, and Lawrence was the subject of some of Winston's writing.

Winston got to know Lawrence of Arabia
and they became friends

On his way back to Britain from Cairo, Winston visited Jerusalem. He always cared about protecting the Jewish population and pushed for a Jewish home state, something that did not happen until the creation of Israel in 1948.

In 1924, Winston was appointed Chancellor of the Exchequer, the highest position his father had attained before him. Winston changed from the Liberal back to the Conservative Party. He never much liked the party system. He had not expected to be offered such a high position, so he was flattered and accepted it. Although Winston did well with money matters, which his new job required, he would rather work with the military. He felt he could better communicate with the military and accomplish more. Working in the treasury was not his forte.

Chapter 9
WWII & Prime Minister

On June 29, 1921, Winston's mother died from a fall. She was sixty-seven years old. Two months later, Winston lost his daughter Marigold at only two years old. A good friend Winston had made in America, Borke Cokran, also died in 1923 at age sixty-nine.

In 1929, the Conservative government was defeated by the Labour Party. Over the next few years, Winston was at odds with Conservatives over various political issues, and they distrustfully eyed his relationships with people of supposedly questionable character.

The years from 1932 to 1936 were hard times. In these five years, Winston's usual good fortune took a vacation. He was a lone wolf, ousted to the political wilderness. His party had been voted out. He had invested in the stock market and lost money in the 1929 crash.

Because Winston was unfamiliar with American traffic lights,
he stepped out of his taxi into the path of a car
and was severely injured

So, Winston went to America to give speeches. His speaking tour was delayed because he was severely injured in December in New York City when he stepped out of his taxi and a car hit him. During the ride, he had been impatiently waiting for unfamiliar traffic lights. Britain did not have such signals until the late 1930s.

Winston's injuries kept him in the hospital. Winston was gloomy, but the distraught driver who had hit Winston asked to see him. Winston permitted the driver to come to his room. The driver had recently become unemployed, but would not take any money when Winston offered it to him.

Characteristically, Winston displayed no animosity, saying it was his own fault since he had been looking the wrong way as vehicles are driven on the other side of the road in Britain, and he did not press any formal charges. It took him a long time to heal, but he eventually recovered and started again. He was not defeated. He wrote about his accident which he sent to the *Daily Mail*. He was paid £600, and the article was read worldwide.

To make up for his loss in the stock market, he tried even harder to get more money for his speaking engagements and book contracts. Winston concentrated on writing during this time.

Winston researched to write his books by reading other books and talking to and working with experts. Winston also travelled to places that he wrote about in his books. There was no instant way to look up information and no computers. Everything had to be written by hand and typed on a typewriter.

In the age before computers were popular,
Winston wrote his books on a typewriter

Winston's memoir *My Early Life* was published in 1930. He wrote *Marlborough: His Life and Times,* a biography about his grandfather that was published in four volumes from 1933 to 1938.

Winston also wrote pieces that later became *Great Contemporaries*, published in 1937, and *A History of the English Speaking Peoples* (four volumes) which was published later in the 1950s. In this time period, he also wrote articles and speeches. He became a well-known and highly paid writer.

Politically, he made a number of blunders and seemed to misstep continually. He supported King Edward VIII, who wanted to marry twice-divorced American commoner Wallis Warfield Simpson. It was against the rules, the moral code, for Edward to marry a commoner and divorcée. She was not an acceptable candidate for queen.

Winston was one of the few politicians to support him, saying Edward was of strong character, so Winston was again on the outside. He tried to get the then Prime Minister Baldwin to stall on making a decision. Many felt that Edward's brother would make a better king anyway. Baldwin gave Edward a few choices. Edward chose to give up the throne. On Dec. 11, 1936, after not even a year of being King, Edward's brother Albert, the Duke of York, became King George VI. Edward then left Britain and married Wallis. It is not certain why Winston supported Edward so strongly. Most believe it was simply because he liked Edward as a person. King George, a more serious person with little sense of humor, was not as fond of Winston as his brother was.

Although Winston might have appeared to be in exile politically, he was still very active and in the public eye. He had friends in the government and was consulted on government issues. Many viewed Winston as a possible leader waiting offstage.

Winston supported King Edward when he desired to marry an American divorcée

By the early 1930s, Germany became a real threat to Britain and the world. The Nazi party had been gaining ground for a decade. Nazi party members went after the young and tried to teach them about the party. On paper, the Nazi party sounded interesting and promising to many disheartened German people. Hitler was a nightmare disguised as a dream. Winston understood how dangerous he was and sounded a warning. In the early 1930s, Winston alerted the British Parliament and the Western world of the threat of the Nazis and that Hitler would start a war.

In 1933, Hitler had become Chancellor of Germany. The British were war-weary from WWI and focused on issues in their own country. Winston continued to speak about it, but he was largely ignored. Winston also warned about the Nazi persecution of Jewish people.

The Parliament continued to favor appeasement, even in the face of Hitler's increasing demands. Winston did not underestimate the threat of Hitler. Armed with insight and experience, he had a knack for analyzing and judging people and situations. Even though Winston was seen by many British as a wise man, his repeated warnings were nevertheless discounted by those in government. The British wanted to avoid war, a sentiment shared with Americans whose distance from Europe kept them even more removed.

In addition to first-hand experience, Winston had studied history and patterns in it intently and passionately. He read widely and remembered what he read, gaining great knowledge of many countries and their people. Doing this helped him to not repeat mistakes made in the past.

It was very late before everyone realized what was happening. Had Winston's warnings been acted upon, it may have been possible to stop Hitler before he built up the German military. A full-scale war possibly could have been avoided.

Britain's Prime Minister Neville Chamberlain met with Hitler for the last time on September 30, 1938 and announced, "My good friends, for the second time in our history, a British Prime

Minister has returned from Germany bringing peace with honor. I believe it is peace for our time . . . Go home and get a nice quiet sleep." Unfortunately, the British would not have long to sleep quietly.

Early on, Winston proclaimed the threat
Hitler presented to the world

On August 23, 1939, Russia signed a nonaggression treaty, the Molotov-Ribbentrop

Pact, with Germany, dividing up Poland. However, Hitler broke the pact and on September 1, 1939, he invaded Poland. When the attack happened, the Polish Ambassador did not call the Prime Minister, but called Winston, who passed on the news. Chamberlain wanted to try to negotiate once more with Hitler. This time, an ultimatum was insisted upon by the British government. Hitler did not give an answer, so Britain declared war on Germany on September 3, 1939.

A national campaign in Britain had begun to bring back Winston. The people thought only Winston could confront Hitler. In 1939, right after Britain had declared war on Germany, Winston was appointed First Lord of the Admiralty for the second time. Shortly thereafter, he was offered a new job, one for which he had been preparing most of his life: Prime Minister.

Some people did not see Winston as Prime Minister material. Nevertheless, he was the right man at the right time. Winston now lived at the famous address, 10 Downing Street in London,

England. He would steer Britain through perilous darkness to victory and light. Winston's love for his country and mankind was clear in his speeches. He crammed days of work into one day. Winston's energy was inexhaustable.

Prime Minister Neville Chamberlain
tried to appease Hitler to no avail

He did not just observe from far away. He was seen everywhere, actively involved in all it took to defeat Hitler. Much was happening elsewhere too. Italy declared war on Britain in June 1940. Japan was about to join forces with Germany. The United States was still not involved.

10 Downing Street is the home of Britain's Prime Minister

Hitler had plans to go after Britain. He had to defeat their Air Force. Britain's Navy was not in good shape, and the Germans had the U-boats that were destroying Britain's maritime supply chain. Winston worked hard to strengthen the Navy.

Winston began to make many of his now famous speeches. Winston remarkably imagined that Britain could fight off fascism, even alone. He passionately conveyed this noble vision to the British people, so they too believed.

In his first speech to The House of Commons as Prime Minister, he gave a strong appeal to action:

"We have before us many, many long months of struggle and of suffering. You ask, what is our policy? I will say: It is to wage war, by sea, land and air, with all our might and with all the strength that God can give us; to wage war against a monstrous tyranny, never surpassed in the dark, and lamentable catalogue of human crime. That is our policy.

"You ask, what is our aim? I can answer in one word: victory. Victory at all costs. Victory in spite of all terror. Victory however long and hard the road may be; for without victory, there is no survival."

A month later on June 4, 1940, he delivered to The House of Commons his "We Shall Fight on the Beaches" speech. The German Army had successfully invaded southern France. Winston talked about the state of the war, and spoke in a manner to boost morale while also sending a plea to the United States for help. He ended with:

"We shall go on to the end. We shall fight in France. We shall fight on the seas and oceans. We shall fight with growing confidence and growing strength in the air. We shall defend our Island, whatever the cost may be, we shall fight on the beaches. We shall fight on the landing grounds. We shall fight in the fields and in the streets. We shall fight in the hills; we shall never surrender."

On June 18, Winston broadcast a message that is often quoted; in particular, the last sentence:

"Let us therefore brace ourselves to our duties, and so bear ourselves that, if the British Empire and its Commonwealth last for a thousand years, men will still say, 'This was their finest hour.'"

Four days later, France surrendered and fell. Britain was alone to face Germany.

Even after France was invaded, Winston refused to negotiate an agreement with Germany. Hitler shortly thereafter attacked and bombed London. This went on through the summer and fall of 1940. In those months, sixty percent of London was destroyed in the bombing raids called "The Blitz." Britain's Royal Air Force defeated the German Air Force (Luftwaffe) and kept German troops from invading on the ground. Britain was badly hurt, but defeating Germany in the air was a turning point in the war.

The public loved Winston, and he was often greeted on the streets. During the German bombing of London, Winston was out in the neighborhoods. He wanted to see what was happening firsthand whether on a battlefield or in the streets. He never wanted to just sit behind a desk. Winston was an emotional person whose feelings showed on his face. He tried to hold back tears, but if he could not, he was not ashamed to shed them.

The British air force defeated the German air force,
preventing a ground invasion

Winston always adhered to checks and balances and had open communication with the House of Commons and the British people. The power of his position did not change his character. While not everyone agreed with him, it was hard not to like him. He would even counter hateful and hurtful comments said to him with a funny comeback or a joke. He did not answer nastiness with more nastiness.

Winston was running a powerful country and trying to keep it intact through difficult times. The fate of Britain was unknown, but Winston was still thoughtful and thankful to those around him. Winston felt comfort from his family, especially his wife and daughters, and enjoyed having them around him. Chartwell was a real refuge, especially in this time of war.

Winston was deeply pained by the destruction of London and its effect on the British people

In 1940, Winston was photographed with a Thompson sub-machine gun, "tommy gun," from America. He posed like a gangster. This photo was used against Winston by Hitler and Winston's critics to push the idea he was a war monger.

Contrary to how he sometimes was portrayed, Winston was decidedly not a war monger. He was not a proponent of war, but if there was to be one, his country needed to be prepared. In his eyes, losing a war was not an option. He believed in the British Empire and retaining its territories, but he also spoke out about those who were treated unfairly or wronged. He saw firsthand and understood the horrors and senselessness of war. Winston always preferred talking to war, but would fight to win if war was inevitable.

Winston posed with an American sub-machine gun, but the photo was used against him by his critics and enemies

Chapter 10
U.S. & WWII

Most European countries entered the war in 1939, when Germany and Russia subdivided Poland. Winston wanted America to enter the war in 1939. Americans did not want to go; it had only been twenty years since the end of WWI. The President of the United States, Franklin Delano Roosevelt, and the United States Congress didn't want to get involved; Roosevelt didn't have the support of the people to enter into a foreign war. He did as much as he could to help Winston rearm Britain instead.

On March 11, 1941, the Lend-Lease Act was passed. Roosevelt could not commit to joining the war, but he could give Britain old military equipment. In return, Britain gave the United States access to bases all over the world. This was useful to the United States. Roosevelt knew that America could get embroiled in the war, and the bases would help if that happened.

On October 29, 1941, Winston gave a talk at Harrow, his former school. He spoke about how Britain had been alone fighting the enemy and persevered. His words are still relevant for today's statesmen and all democratic citizens:

"Never give in—never, never, never, never—in nothing great or small, large or petty, never give in except to convictions of honor and good sense. Never yield to force; never yield to the apparently overwhelming might of the enemy."

Winston tried to act as he spoke. He refused to back down and kept a close eye on Germany and the other European Axis countries. Meanwhile, Japan invaded Southeast Asia in a quest for natural resources including rubber and oil. Japan had been moving for years into Korea and down through China. Japan wanted to control all of Asia. To do that, Japan needed to eliminate the possibility of the United States' military interfering in their plan.

On December 7, 1941, the Japanese attacked the naval base at Pearl Harbor in Hawaii. A day

Honolulu Star-Bulletin 1ST EXTRA

8 PAGES HONOLULU, TERRITORY OF HAWAII, U.S.A SUNDAY, DECEMBER 7, 1941 8 PAGES   FIVE CENTS

WAR!

(ASSOCIATED PRESS BY TRANSPACIFIC TELEPHONE)

SAN FRANCISCO, DEC. 7

PRESIDENT ROOSEVELT ANNOUNCED THIS MORNING THAT JAPANESE PLANES HAD ATTACKED MANILA AND PEARL HARBOR.

OAHU BOMBED BY JAPANESE PLANES

America entered the war after Japanese
planes bombed Pearl Harbor

later, the U.S. declared war on Japan. The United States was now in the war. The Japanese attack pushed the United States into the war. Winston wished something less drastic and agonizing had paved the way for the United States to join with Great Britain.

Britain needed America's military production ability and troops to fight Hitler's Germany. Britain did not have the quantity that was needed. Their production was not small, by any means, but America could exceed Britain by the sheer amount of manpower. The Great Depression was ending, and the war helped the American economy by putting people back to work.

When Hitler invaded the Soviet Union, Joseph Stalin, its leader, joined with the Allies. Winston and Roosevelt were leery of this joint venture with the communist Soviet Union, but they needed its military strength. Winston managed to deftly handle Roosevelt and Stalin. Roosevelt did not understand the dangers of communism as Winston did, who had experienced it firsthand. As the war progressed, Winston wanted to keep the Allies—Britain, the United States, and the Soviet Union—glued together.

He was genuinely friends with Roosevelt and they enjoyed each other's company. With Joseph Stalin, an unsuitable but necessary associate, Winston danced carefully. Winston really did not have a choice: he had to make Stalin an ally in order to defeat Hitler.

Winston also needed to figure out Germany's plans. They used a machine called an Enigma machine to encode and decode their messages.

Franklin Delano Roosevelt and Winston Churchill
enjoyed a genuine friendship

The Allied forces couldn't figure out what the
messages said, so they never knew what the Axis
powers were going to do next. After an Enigma
machine was confiscated off a destroyed
German U-boat, a top-secret intelligence group
began trying to decode the machine. Getting the
enemy's secrets was a key to turning the war in
the favor of the Allies. A mathematician, Alan
Turing, designed a computer to decode the
Enigma messages. Soon, the Allies could read
every message Germany sent.

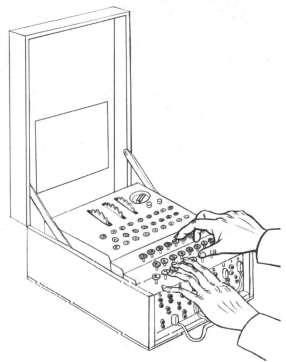

A German Enigma machine was found by the British,
and was secretly used to decode German messages
that helped to win the war

Winston met with President Roosevelt and
went to The White House often during the war.
He was proud to be half-American and had a
great love for the country. Winston always
wanted Britain to have a strong relationship with
America. Despite the Revolutionary War when
America fought Britain for its independence, the
two countries became great allies.

In December of 1941, Winston came to America to discuss military strategy. On December 26, he addressed a joint session of Congress. He teasingly told the House and Senate, "If my father had been American and my mother British, instead of the other way 'round, I might have got here on my own!" That night, Winston stayed overnight in the White House in the Lincoln bedroom and it is rumored that he saw Lincoln's ghost. Supposedly he also had a mild heart attack during his stay in America, but he did not stop his rigorous schedule.

Winston eloquently addressed Congress
shortly after Pearl Harbor

Nearly a month later, in January 1942, he and Lord Beaverbrook, Winston's friend and Minister of Supply, flew back to Britain. Such high level leaders were not supposed to fly on the same plane, according to the British King. The two men had not followed the King's orders. However, only Lord Beaverbrook seemed to grasp the seriousness of their mistake at this time of world crisis. At night on the plane Lord Beaverbrook told the pilot in private, "If we lose Churchill, we lose the war."

The primary Allied leaders, Churchill, Roosevelt, and Stalin, met at Yalta to discuss the end of the war

Toward the end of the war in February of 1945, Winston, Roosevelt and Joseph Stalin met in Yalta, a city in the Soviet Union. They discussed strategy and what would happen when the war ended. Each came up with his own plan. Winston was still much more skeptical and cautious of Stalin's agreements than was President Roosevelt.

On April 12, 1945, President Roosevelt died from a stroke. He had been in declining health, but Winston was shocked to hear the news. Winston gave a eulogy for Roosevelt in the House of Commons.

Vice-President Harry Truman was now President of the United States. Winston found Truman clear-sighted, knowledgeable, and easier in many ways to deal with than Roosevelt.

After six exhausting years of war, Germany surrendered on May 7, 1945. Hitler committed suicide, and Winston was thankful because he did not look forward to having to execute him. World War II was not just a war between a few countries. Twenty-six countries were combatants, and about sixty million people died in Asia, Africa, Europe, and Australia.

After Roosevelt died, Harry Truman became President, and he and Winston liked each other and had a strong alliance

In response to the mass murder of the Jews by the Nazis, Winston said, "There is no doubt that this is probably the greatest and most horrible crime ever committed in the whole history of the world." Leading his country during these years had taken its toll on Winston. Winston celebrated the end of the war and gave many speeches.

Most historians of note claim that Winston saved Britain and almost certainly the world from utter destruction. Winston got Britain through the war, but his party was defeated in the 1945 election, so Winston was out of office. The British people did not want Winston's party in power after the war ended.

Winston celebrated VE Day with the Queen and the rest of the royal family

Chapter 11
Post-WWII & Death

Although Winston was not reelected as Prime Minister, he had plenty of work to do. He had books to write, speeches to give, art to paint, and travels to make. He was upset at first about being replaced, but in time he saw it as a positive change in his life.

America revered and respected Winston, so he headed to its shores. He gave speeches about the Soviet Union and warned the Americans about Stalin and the dangers of communism. Winston had long ago spoken out against communism. He believed communism took away individual freedoms and gave too much power to the government.

Like fascism, communism repressed people's rights, and the government controlled people's lives. Winston never let up on his fight for the cause of democracy. He knew it had to be protected and nurtured. Freedom was not free.

He wanted to be sure that America and Britain, in particular, would always be diligent to preserve freedom and democracy.

Winston gave his famous "Iron Curtain" speech at Westminster College in Fulton, Missouri on March 5, 1946. Winston probably coined the terms "Cold War" and "Iron Curtain." He said an Iron Curtain had fallen over Europe and Stalin planned to spread Communism in Europe. Eventually, it would invade America. He was sounding another warning.

In October 1951, Winston was elected Prime Minister again, now as a Conservative. He focused primarily on issues within the country. He also focused on keeping the British relationship strong with the United States.

In 1953, Winston won the Nobel Prize for Literature. He received this esteemed prize for his six-volume book *The Second World War*. The Nobel Prize points to his fame as an author, historian, and artist. The prize committee even paid tribute to his gift of speech. In the same year, Winston accepted the highest order of chivalry given to a commoner, Knight Companion of the Order of the Garter, awarded to him by the Queen of England and the British Empire, Elizabeth II. He had always avoided that kind of honor because he wanted to remain *Mr.* Winston Churchill. Now he had to change his name to *Sir* Winston Churchill.

Winston was slowing down, but he still functioned quite well, despite a stroke. In 1955 at age seventy-nine, he resigned as Prime

Winston avoided honors and titles for most of his life, but finally accepted being knighted by the Queen

Minister, although he kept his seat in The House of Commons nearly up to the time he died.

As he got older, Winston's love of animals was especially apparent. Despite his gruff demeanor, he was really soft-hearted and treasured his furry companions. He also wrote thoughtful notes to the people who cared for his pets when he was away. His poodle Rufus died in 1947 after being hit by a car. The loss was painful for Winston, but then he was given another poodle named Rufus II shortly after. Winston always said the "II" after Rufus was silent.

Winston also loved cats and had a number of them. Once he yelled at one of his cats, who then ran away for a few days. Winston posted a sign on a window: "all is forgiven." In honor of Jock, a cat who shared his later years, Winston requested there always be an orange cat with a white chest and four white paws at Chartwell. His wish continues to be honored today. Chartwell is now a well-preserved tourist site, a national treasure. Admiring visitors greet the lucky, well-loved cat who lives in plush accommodations on spectacular grounds with plenty of places to hide and play.

The Chartwell cat enjoys sunning itself on Winston's statue

On January 15, 1965, Winston fell while staying in Monte Carlo, France, and quickly returned to Britain. His health steadily declined thereafter. Winston died from a stroke at age ninety on January 24, 1965, seventy years after his father on the exact same day. He died peacefully and surrounded by his family. Although they were sad, Winston was ready to go.

Winston and Clementine had a successful marriage
that lasted until Winston's death parted them

The world mourned Winston's death. Hundreds of thousands of people came to see his coffin and pay their respects in Westminster Hall in London. The Queen gave Winston a State Funeral, calling Winston "a national hero." Such a funeral had not been decreed for a commoner for over a century. On January 30, 1965, people all over the world sat in front of their televisions to watch Winston Churchill's funeral. At the time it was the largest state funeral ever seen. He was buried in a churchyard near Blenheim Palace. Winston had come full circle back to the place where he had been born.

Winston was survived by his wife and his children Mary, Sarah, and only son Randolph. Winston loved, cared, and worried about his children, and they greatly admired him.

Winston left behind a large family including many grandchildren

It probably was not always easy having a father of Winston's stature. His children had many accomplishments, yet all had lives with ongoing troubles. Except for his youngest daughter, Mary Soames, who died at age ninety-one, Winston's children all died relatively young. Marigold died as a toddler. Diana died in 1963, two years before her father's death. Randolph died of a heart attack three years after his father. Sarah died in 1982. The family is buried together near Blenheim Palace.

Winston left behind ten grandchildren, and numerous great-grandchildren. Winston Jr., Winston's grandson, has said that Winston was a caring grandfather. Winston Jr. liked to stay at Chartwell, and his grandfather wrote him long letters when he was in boarding school. He got lots of attention from his grandparents, and Winston eased his loneliness while at school.

Winston was given a State Funeral by the Queen, and people all over the world watched it on television

Celia Sandys, Winston's granddaughter (daughter of Diana), has written books about Winston and made a documentary called *Chasing Churchill: In Search of My Grandfather*. It is a loving portrait of him and his travels around the world. She also gives lectures on her famous grandfather, and is a trustee of The Churchill Centre.

Winston's granddaughter has written books about her famous grandfather and made a documentary about his travels

Churchill's legacy lives today in his words, paintings, foundations, and institutions. Churchill College at Cambridge, which was established in commemoration of Winston, was set up primarily for the study of science and technology. Winston saw technology as important for the future of Britain.

Much of what Winston foresaw would become eventualities, such as the importance and growth of technology, a future energy crisis, and, as early as 1905, the formation of an Israeli state. In his lifetime, he foresaw WWI, German expansionism, WWII, and the rise of Communism. Today, many of Winston's warnings are still relevant.

No matter what times you live in, a country needs a leader with strength, character, and integrity. They need to be able to look forward and embrace change while still revering traditions and founding principles. Winston was not stagnant; he was able to alter his views and evolve with the times. He was not afraid to tell people what was difficult to hear. He did not sugarcoat, sidestep, or ignore any clear threats or danger threatening democracy and freedom. Many people today look for the return of forthright statesmen like Winston.

Select Quotes from Winston Churchill

"We have before us many, many long months of struggle and of suffering. You ask, what is our policy? I can say: It is to wage war, by sea, land and air, with all our might and with all the strength that God can give us; to wage war against a monstrous tyranny, never surpassed in the dark, lamentable catalogue of human crime. That is our policy.

You ask, what is our aim? I can answer in one word: It is victory, victory at all costs, victory in spite of all terror, victory, however long and hard the road may be; for without victory, there is no survival."

– Excerpt from Churchill's first speech as
Prime Minister, May 13, 1940

"There is no doubt that this is probably the greatest and most horrible crime ever committed in the whole history of the world."

– Churchill's assessment of the Holocaust

Winston Churchill Timeline

1874 November 30   Born in Oxfordshire, England at Blenheim Palace

1882   Begins attending St. George's

1884   Leaves St. George's for Misses Thompsons' Preparatory School in Brighton

1888   Begins attending Harrow School near London

1893   Attends Sandhurst

1894   Graduates Sandhurst

1895 January 24   His father, Lord Randolph Churchill dies

1895 March   Assigned to the Army Regiment, the 4th Hussars; Becomes war correspondent/officer

1899   First run (a loss) for Parliament

1899 November 15   Captured by the Boers and escapes

1900   Wins a seat in the House of Commons; Gives lecture tour in America

1908 September 12   Marries Clementine Hozier

1909   Daughter Diana is born

1911   Son Randolph is born

1911   Becomes First Lord of the Admiralty

1914   Daughter Sarah is born

1917   Becomes Minister of Munitions

1918   Daughter Marigold is born

1921 June 29   Mother, Lady Randolph Churchill (Jennie Jerome) dies

1921 August 23   Marigold dies from septicemia

World Timeline

1885 First gasoline powered automobile invented

1892 Sherlock Holmes first published

1893 January Labour Party holds first meeting

1896 September 22 Queen Victoria becomes the longest-reigning British monarch

1887 January Lord Randolph Churchill resigns from Parliament

1899 Second Boer war begins

1901 Queen Victoria dies; Edward VII becomes King of England

1910 George V becomes King

1912 Titanic sinks

1914 Archduke assassinated, Britain declares war on Germany, beginning WWI

1915 April 25 Gallipoli Campaign causes many casualties

1917 United States declares war on Germany

1918 Armistice ends WWI

1919 Treaty of Versailles redraws Europe's borders

1922 British Empire is at its largest, ruling over 25% of the Earth's population

1924 Troops begin withdrawing from Germany

1929 Stock market crash

1933 Hitler becomes dictator of Germany

1936 Edward VIII becomes King then gives up the throne; Albert, the Duke of York, becomes King George VI

Winston Churchill Timeline (cont.)

1922   Daughter Mary born; Buys Chartwell

1924   Becomes Chancellor of the Exchequer

1940 May   Elected Prime Minister

1941 December 26   Addresses U.S. Congress

1945 February   Meets with Roosevelt and Stalin
in Yalta

1945 May 8   WWII ends in Europe

1945 July   Loses reelection for Prime Minister

1951 October   Elected Prime Minster the second time

1953   Awarded the Nobel Prize for Literature

1955   Retires as Prime Minister

1963   Made an honorary citizen of the U.S.

1965 January 24   Dies from a stroke in England;
Buried in a churchyard near Blenheim Palace

World Timeline (cont.)

1939 September 1   Germany invades Poland; WWII begins

1940   Battle of Britain

1941 December 7   The Japanese attack Pearl Harbor

1945 April 12   President Roosevelt dies; Harry S. Truman swears in

1945 May 7   Germany surrenders; WWII ends in Europe

1953   Elizabeth II becomes Queen

1955   Dr. Jonas Salk vaccinates 500,000 people against polio in Britain

1963   Harold MacMillan, the Prime Minister after Winston, resigns

Glossary

10 Downing Street   Official residence and office address of the British Prime Minister; similar to the White House for US Presidents

Accolades   Honor or praise. In the environment of Sandhurst this would be for battle maneuvers and drills, walking, riding, and soldiering on horseback

Allies World War II (1939–1945)   The countries fighting against Nazi Germany. The main four were: Great Britain, The United States, The Soviet Union / Russia, and France

Appeasement   A policy that promotes giving in even when it is wrong to do so to preserve peace or calm

Archduke   A position in Austrian monarchy between a Prince and a King

Battle of Britain   Summer and fall 1940 during World War II. German Air Force operation against Britain's Air Force. First major battle fought entirely by air forces

Blitz   Germany's relentless bombing of Britain. Notable because Germany did not destroy Britain's air force and Britain did not yield, negotiate, or surrender. A major turning point in WWII in Britain's favor

Bolshevik   The communist party that seized power during the Russian Revolution

Bureaucracy   A system of government organized by strictly following a set routine or procedure

Chancellor of the Exchequer   Head of the treasury of Great Britain

Chartwell   Winston Churchill's home in Kent

Communist A system of government where the government controls all property and goods and everything is shared among the people

Confidante A person secrets are told to

Conservative Party A political party in the United Kingdom that focuses on low taxes, free trade, and less rules for businesses

Correspondent a journalist who is on location and reports for a newspaper or magazine

Czar Russian for emperor. The ruler of Russia until the 1917 Bolshevik Revolution

Dardanelles Campaign April 25, 1915 to January 9, 1916. Sea and land attack on the Dardanelles strait in Gallipoli Peninsula in Turkey

Deficient Not up to a normal standard

Enigma Machine A machine used to encode German messages during World War II

Fascism A system of government headed by a dictator in which the government controls business and work, and protest is not allowed

First Lord of the Admiralty Head of the British Royal Navy

Forte A person's strong point or specialty; something someone does very well

High Church A formal church with traditional rituals and beliefs

HMS An abbreviation for Her Majesty's Ship; a designation that a ship is part of the British Royal Navy

House of Commons Democratically elected body. Members of Parliament represent voter's interests and concerns. Operates similar to the US House of Representatives

Lend-Lease Act   March 11, 1941. Permitted the United States to lend or lease military supplies to Allies fighting Germany. This was primarily to help Great Britain with supplies, and the U.S. could remain neutral but prepared for war

Liberal Party   A political party in the United Kingdom that focused on welfare reform. This party led the UK through WWII

Low Church   A church that does not emphasis rituals, sacraments, or clergyman

Maritime   Relating to the sea or boating

Order of Chivalry   A group of knights. A person must get an Order of Chivalry to become a knight

Parliament   Assembly of representatives that makes laws. In Britain, it is made up of the House of Commons and House of Lords

Precocious   Showing qualities or abilities of an adult while still a child

Prime Minister   Leader of the British government

Regiment   A military unit, usually with a set number of soldiers under a commander. Also called a battalion or company

Revered   To show honor, respect, or devotion to something

Septicemia   A fatal infection of the blood

Solace   Comfort during worrying or grief

Squalid   Filthy, neglected, or run-down due to a lack of money

Stagnant   Not active

U-boat   Shortened English version of the German *Unterseeboot* or submarine.

Vindicate   To free from blame or guilt

Warmonger   Someone who pushes for and stirs up war

Bibliography

Churchill, Winston S. *My Early Life: A Roving Commission*. NY: Charles Scribner's Sons, 1930, renewal 1958.

Gilbert, Martin. *Churchill: A Life*. NY: Henry Holt & Co., 1991

Gilbert, Martin. *Winston Churchill : The Wilderness Years*. Boston: Houghton Mifflin Company, 1982

Johnson, Paul. *Churchill*. NY: Viking, 2009. 1st edition

Pilpel, Robert. *Churchill in America 1895-1961: An Affectionate Portrait*. New York & London: HBJ, 1976

Sandys, Celia. *Chasing Churchill: The Travels of Winston Churchill*. NY: Carroll & Graf, 2003. HB; NY: Basic Books, 2004. PB.

Chasing Churchill. 2003. DVD. Presented by Celia Sandys. Dir. Stephen Moore

Winston Churchill. A&E Home Video, 2003. DVD. Box set.

Index

A

attack through the Dardanelles, 55, 56
Austria-Hungary, 53

B

Battle of Omdurman (1878), 34
The Blitz, 78
Bolshevik Revolution, 60
Boston, Massachusetts, 40
Boston Herald, 40
Brabazon (Colonel), 25, 28
British Army. *See also* military career
    Fourth Hussars, 28
    resignation from, 34
    war correspondent, 29–38

C

Cape Colony, South Africa, 35, 36, 37
captured in South Africa, 36, 37, 38
Chamberlain, Neville, 71, 73, 74
Chancellor of the Exchequer
    Churchill, Winston, 62
    George, Lloyd, 49, 50
    Randolph (Lord), 14
Chant, Laura Ormiston, 21, 23
Chartwell, 47, 80, 96
Churchill, Clementine (wife)
    children of, 46
    dislike of Winston's friends, 50
Churchill, Diana (daughter), 46
Churchill, John (brother), 8, 9, 17, 18
Churchill, Marigold (daughter), 46
Churchill, Mary (daughter), 46, 47
Churchill, Randolph (father), 1, 2, 4, 5, 13, 14
    death of, 25, 26, 27
Churchill, Randolph (son), 46
Churchill, Sarah (daughter), 46
Churchill, Winston

Index (cont.)

    asking United States for help, 77
    attack through the Dardanelles, 55, 56
    birth of, 1
    as cavalry officer, 25, 26
    captured in South Africa, 36, 37, 38
    Chancellor of the Exchequer, 62
    as civilian journalist, 35
    death of, 98, 99, 100, 101
    demoted from Admiralty, 56
    early childhood of, 1–9
    education, 3, 4, 6 (*See also* education)
    elected Prime Minister (1930), 94
    end of World War II, 91, 92
    first official speech, 23
    first speech as Prime Minister, 76–77
    injured in New York City (NY), 65, 66
    legacy, 101, 102
    marriage, 45, 46
    Middle East policy, 61
    Minister of Munitions, 59
    move to Chartwell, 46, 47
    Oldham district House of Commons victory (1880), 38
    post-WWII, 94–105
    as Prime Minister (during WWII), 74–81
    rising star in politics, 48–53
    as soldier in Flanders, 57, 58
    as statesman, 39–42
    as war correspondent, 29–38
    World War I, 54–58
    World War II, 64–82
    in Yalta, 90, 91
civilian journalist, 35
Cockran, Bourke, 64
Conservative Party
    Oldham district victory (1880), 38
    switch back to (1904), 63
    switch to Liberal Party (1884), 48
cramming schools, 18
Cuba

Index (cont.)

cigars, 32
fight against rebels, 31
as war correspondent in, 29, 33

D

Daily Graphic, 29. *See also* war correspondent
Daily Mail, 66
Daily Telegraph, 21
depression, 56
Dublin, Ireland, 2, 3
Duke of Marlborough, 1, 3

E

early childhood, 1–9
education, 3, 4, 6, 10–28
    cramming schools, 18
    Harrow School, 13, 14, 15, 16
    Royal Military Academy, Sandhurst (RMAS), 18, 19, 20, 24
    St. George's School, 10, 11, 12
Edward VIII (King), 68, 69
Egypt
    Battle of Omdurman (1878), 34
    as war correspondent in, 33, 34
The Enchantress, 51
Enigma Machine, 85, 86, 87
The Entertainments Protection League, 21
Eton College, 13
Everest, Elizabeth. (nanny), 7, 8, 9, 28

F

Ferdinand, Franz, 53
First Lord of the Admiralty, 51, 54, 56
    appointment for second time, 73
Fourth Hussars, 28
France
    entry into World War I, 53
    German invasion of (1920), 77
    study of military, 52
    surrender of to Germany, 78
friends

Index (cont.)

Lawrence, T.E., 61, 62
The Other Club, 50, 51

G

Gallipoli Peninsula (Turkey), 55, 56
George, Lloyd, 49, 59
    attack through the Dardanelles, 55, 56
George VI (King), 68, 69
German Air Force (Luftwaffe), 78
Germany, 70. *See also* wars
    bombing London, England, 78, 79, 80
    Enigma Machine, 86, 87, 88
    France surrender to, 78
    Great Britain war with (1919), 73
    invasion of Poland (1919), 73
    invasion of Soviet Union (1921), 85
    Molotov-Ribbentrop Pact (1919), 72
Great Britain
    Churchill as Prime Minister (during WW II), 74–81
    entry into World War I, 53
    Italy declaration of war on (Great 1920), 75
    Khyber Pass, 32
    United States during WW II, 83–93
    war with Germany (1919), 73
Great Contemporaries (Churchill), 67

H

Harrow School, 13, 14, 15, 16, 83
health
    depression, 56
    at St. George's School, 12
History of the English Speaking Peoples (Churchill), 67
Hitler, Adolf, 60, 70, 71, 75, vii. *See also* wars
    bombing London, England, 78, 79, 80
    Chamberlain's meeting with (1918), 72
    death of, 91
    Great Britain war with Germany (1919), 73
    invasion of Poland (1919), 73
    invasion of Soviet Union (1921), 85

Index (cont.)

HMS Eurydice, sinking of, 4, 5
House of Commons
    Churchill's first speech as Prime Minister, 76–77
    Oldham district victory (1880), 39
Hozier, Clementine (wife), 42, 43, 44. *See also* Churchill, Clementine
    (wife)
    marriage, 45, 46
    proposal to, 45

I

India, 32, 33
Industrial Revolution, 52
Iron Curtain speech (1926), 95
Italy, declaration of war (1920), 75

J

Japan
    invasion of Southeast Asia (1921), 84
    Pearl Harbor attack (1921), 84, 85
Jerome, Jennie (mother), 1, 2, 4, 8

K

Khyber Pass, 32
Knight Companion of the Order of the Garter, 95

L

Lawrence, T.E., 61, 62
legacy, 101, 102
Lend-Lease Act (1921), 82
Liberal Party
    switch from (1904), 63
    switch to (1884), 48
London, England, bombing during WW II, 78, 79, 80
Luftwaffe (German Air Force), 78

M

Marlborough: His Life and Times (Churchill), 67
Middle East policy, 61
military career, 12, 25, 26
    fight against Cuban rebels, 31

Index (cont.)

First Lord of the Admiralty, 51, 54, 56
Fourth Hussars, 28
as soldier in Flanders, 57, 58
war correspondent, 29–38
Minister of Munitions, 59
Molotov-Ribbentrop Pact (1919), 72
My Early Life (Churchill), 67

N
Navy
attack through the Dardanelles, 55, 56
First Lord of the Admiralty, 51, 54, 56, 73
Nazi party, 70, 71. *See also* wars
bombing London, England, 78, 79, 80
invasion of Poland (1919), 73
invasion of Soviet Union (1921), 85
New York City (NY)
first trip to, 29, 30
injured in, 65, 66
Nobel Prize for Literature (1932), 94

O
The Other Club, 50, 51

P
paid lecture tour (1880), 39, 40
painting, 58
Parliament, 48. *See also* House of Commons; political career
Pearl Harbor attack (1921), 83, 84, 85
political career.
demoted from Admiralty, 56
elected Prime Minister second time (1930), 94
First Lord of the Admiralty, 73
first race for House of Commons, 34
Minister of Munitions, 59
Oldham district House of Commons victory (1880), 38
rising star in politics, 48–53
Prime Minister
Chamberlain, Neville, 72
Churchill as (during WWII), 74–81

Index (cont.)

    Churchill elected second time (1930), 94
    first speech as, 76–77
    George, Lloyd, 59
Purity Campaign, 21, 22

R

The River War (Churchill), 34
Roosevelt, Franklin D. (FDR), 83, 90, 91, vii
Royal Air Force, 78
Royal Military Academy, Sandhurst (RMAS), 18, 19, 20
Russia
    Bolshevik Revolution, 60
    entry into World War I, 53
    Molotov-Ribbentrop Pact (1919), 72

S

Sandhurst. *See* Royal Military Academy, Sandhurst (RMAS)
Second Boer War, 34, 35, 36, 40, 41
The Second World War (Churchill), 94
South Africa, captured in, 35, 36, 37
Soviet Union, 85. *See also* Russia
speeches
    asking United States for help, 77
    first official, 23
    first speech as Prime Minister, 76–77
    Harrow School (1921), 84
    paid lecture tour (1880), 40, 65, 66
Stalin, Josef, 89, 90. *See also* Russia
statesman, Churchill as, 39–42
St. George's School, 10, 11, 12
St. James's School. *See* St. George's School
St. Margaret's Church, Westminster, 44
stock market crash (1909), 64
Sudan, as war correspondent in, 33, 34

T

technology. advancement of, 52, 53
10 Downing Street, 73, 75
The Story of the Malakand Field Force (Churchill), 33
Treasure Island, 11

Index (cont.)

Truman Harry, 90, 91
Twain, Mark, 40, 41

U

United States. *See also* wars
    Churchill's visit to (1921), 88
    Pearl Harbor attack (1921), 83, 84

V

VE Day, 92

W

war correspondent, 29–38
World War I, 53, 54–58
    attack through the Dardanelles, 55, 56
World War II, vii
    asking United States for help, 77
    The Blitz, 78
    bombing London, England, 78, 79, 80
    Churchill, Winston, 64–82
    Churchill as Prime Minister during, 74–81
    end of, 90, 91
    Italy declaration of war (on Great Britain, 1920), 74
    Pearl Harbor attack (1921), 83, 84
    United States, 83–93
writing, 66, 67
    civilian journalist, 35
    war correspondent, 29–38

Y

Yalta, meeting in, 89, 90